Dear Abuelita

Sofía Meza Keane

Illustrated by
Enrique O. Sánchez

Rigby

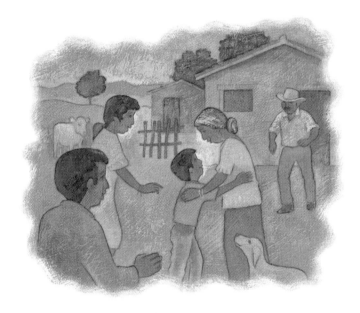

© 1997 by Rigby,
a division of Reed Elsevier Inc.
500 Coventry Lane
Crystal Lake, IL 60014

00 99
10 9 8 7 6 5 4

Printed in Singapore

ISBN 0-7635-3156-1

3

San Jose, June 15

Dear Abuelita,

It's been a week since we arrived in San Jose. We were exhausted from the trip. Papa drove for days. Guess what I saw, Grandma. A roadrunner! I saw it when we crossed the Sonoran desert.

When we arrived in San Jose, we were starving. It was as hot as an oven, and we were hungry. Papa took us to a restaurant that was nice and cool. That was great! The best part was the red racing car that came with my hamburger.

I miss the happiness and noise of the farm. I remember you telling me how the animals seem to talk all the time. You taught me that the roosters crow, the sheep bleat, and the pigs oink. Remember? Here at home everything is just the opposite. Night and day, everything is as quiet as can be.

Grandma, I miss you. Write soon.

Love,
Marco

San Jose, July 5

Dear Abuelita Trini,

How are you? How is everything on the farm? I'm going to tell you all about San Jose. You won't believe it, Grandma, but being in San Jose is like being in another world. The buildings downtown are so tall that when I stand beside them, I feel like a mouse. The most incredible thing was to see the fireworks last night. They looked as if they were falling right on the buildings. Papa told me that the fireworks were for the United States Independence Day.

You know, Grandma, on the farm there aren't any tall buildings or paved streets lit up at night. On the farm, I saw only the stars. Here in San Jose, all the houses, cars, and stores are lit. I'd rather see the stars because they look like candles.

Grandma, I miss you a lot.

Hugs and kisses,
Marco

San Jose, July 17

Dear Abuelita,

I was excited to get your letter yesterday.

Would you like to know about our new house? I'm full of surprising news. The house and the farm are as different as night and day.

Imagine, Grandma! Here we have running water. As soon as you turn on the faucet, nice clear water pours out. It's not the way it was on the farm, where we needed to wait each week for the water truck to come so we could fill our buckets. The first time I took a shower, I didn't want to get out. The water from the shower felt nice and warm. I got out only because I was hungry.

Lots of kisses from San Jose,
Marco

San Jose, July 29

Dear Abuelita Trini,

Yesterday was my birthday. I'm a big kid now—eight years old. Mama made me a cake with strawberry filling, and we drank lots of chocolate milk. The chocolate milk was good, but it didn't taste as good as yours because we didn't make it with Blanquita's milk. Blanquita's milk is the best in the whole world.

What do you think Papa gave me for my birthday? A stuffed toy cow. It's soft and white and has big black eyes. Its name is Blanquita, like my cow on the farm. I'm going to send you a picture of you milking Blanquita. Grandma, even though I had a good time on my birthday, I missed you. I missed all my friends from Yucatán, especially Paquito. Do you know what I miss the most, Grandma? I miss the stories you would tell me before I went to bed.

Grandma, take care.

Till next time,
Marco

San Jose, August 30

Dear Abuelita,

I'm very excited because tomorrow will be my first day at Garner School.

Can you believe this? The school is as big as two soccer fields. It has lots of rooms and playground equipment. Imagine that! It has basketball courts and a field to play baseball on.

The Morelos School had a big playground, but it didn't have swings, slides, or basketball courts. I think this school has twenty rooms. Do you remember the Morelos School? It had only five.

Grandma, I'm a little nervous about school. I'm afraid because I won't know anybody there. Paquito, my best friend, won't be with me. I'm afraid I won't have any friends and the kids will laugh at me.

Even though I like San Jose, I miss the farm. I miss you very much.

Love,
Marco

San Jose, September 12

Dear Abuelita Trini,

Today when I got your letter, I jumped for joy. I'm glad that you and Grandpa are doing fine. I'm not doing so well.

It's been more than a week since I started school. Unfortunately, school isn't as fun as I'd hoped it would be. You can't imagine how weird I felt the first day. When Ms. Gomez introduced me to the class, all the kids just stared at me. I wanted to sink into the ground.

After Ms. Gomez pointed me to my desk, I walked to it as fast as I could. Getting there seemed to take forever. Quickly I sat down, took out my pencil and notebook, and started to write.

The worst part is that I still have no friends. During recess I get bored because I have no one to play with. Grandma, I wish I could be at my old school.

I love you.

Yours,
Marco

Marco

San Jose, September 22

Dear Abuelita Trini,

My adventures with the buses in San Jose are unbelievable.

Imagine, Grandma! The buses are almost new and hardly anybody rides them. They even have air-conditioning. The bus drivers wear uniforms and are nice. They wait until you get off the bus before they take off. On top of that, the buses arrive at the stops on time.

Can you believe this, Grandma? On the farm, we needed to wait for the bus for hours. It was always full, and sometimes it didn't even stop. Do you remember how upset we used to get?

One time when Mama and I rode the bus downtown, we got lost. All the signs are in English. Since we didn't know enough English to understand them or to speak with anybody, we missed our stop. It took us hours to reach downtown.

Grandma, I've already told you everything. Write soon.

Love,
Marco

San Jose, October 9

Dear Abuelita,

    I have wonderful news for you. Can you guess? Come on, Grandma. It's about my new friend, Alex.

    The day I made friends with Alex, I was sitting on the grass, watching the kids play baseball. You wouldn't believe how much I wanted to play. I thought, I have to do something so I can join the game. So I jumped up and asked the kids if I could play. "Sure," said Alex. "Our team needs another player." Soon I was running from base to base.

    Can you believe it, Grandma? Now baseball is my favorite sport. I even hit a home run in that game. All the kids on my team were happy because we'd won. We agreed that from then on, we'd play every day. I wish my friends in Yucatán had seen me. I'm so happy!

             Love and kisses,
             Marco

San Jose, November 3

Dear Abuelita,

How is everything going on the farm? Are you fattening up another pig? I'm sure that if it gets really big, you'll make lots of money when you sell it. You'll see! Do you have enough hay in the barn for the cows to graze this winter? Remember when you taught me about that?

I'm still playing baseball at school. Sometimes I get bored at home because I can't go out and play. You won't believe how much I want to ride Bayo. By the way, how is that horse doing? What about Pinto? Is that big-eared dog as frisky as ever? I remember he always wanted to run as fast as Bayo.

Grandma, I'll write again soon and tell you how things are going. You are always in my thoughts.

Yours,
Marco

San Jose, November 15

Dear Abuelita,

    I have a surprise for you. Would you like to guess? Let's see. I'll give you three chances. No, that's not it. Wrong again. No, not that either. Do you give up? Well, I'll tell you. We're planning to visit you for Christmas. Papa said that we'll be there for a week. I'm so excited! The only thing on my mind is the number of days till vacation.

    Do you remember what I told you about Alex? He's my best friend. I know that I'll miss him when I go to the farm. I'd love for him to go with us. He says that he's never been to a farm. It would be fun to teach him how to ride a horse. But his parents won't let him go. Maybe next time, they say. Too bad!

    I'll see you very, very soon, Grandma.

Your grandson,
who never forgets you,
Marco